The Zenith Venue:

Inside The Mind Of A
Chosen Scholar
(Vol. 1)

B-poet

THE ZENITH VENUE:
Inside The Mind Of A Chosen Scholar (Vol. 1)
Copyright © 2023 **B-poet**

ISBN (Paperback): 978-1-958475-15-7
ISBN (Ebook): 978-1-958475-16-4

Freelance Poetry LLC
Suite #130
5348 Vegas Drive
Las Vegas, NV 89108

Printed in the United States of America.

PROMINENT
BOOKS

5830 E 2nd St, Ste 7000 #9983
Casper, WY 82609
USA

CONTENTS

The Zenith Venue:

Inside The Mind Of A Chosen Scholar (Vol. 1)

B-poet

Discover and explore the *Lost Poetic Archives* along with B-poet's volumed poetry at *Originsofthelostpoeticarchives.godaddysites.com*

WHAT'S NEXT ON THE HORIZON?

If you could look back
In your rearview mirror
As an outsider looking in
What kind of a spin?
Would you place
On your own destiny?
As the sun rises in the east
And sets in the west
What's Next On The Horizon?
For you since life's daily tests
Have beget every personal regret

By not leaving behind
A viewed trace of valued remembrance
As *meaningful* & *humbled* occurrences
Once signified why the mind
Chose nostalgia so
Every forgotten regret
Could finally
Bask in the graciousness
Of yesterdays' scenic
Lake's forgiving sunsets'
Actioned tranquility

LIVING NEAR THE WATER'S EDGE

Sparkling streams of potential dangers
Unseen to the naked eye
Each and *Every* onlooker
Who's been
Living Near The Water's Edge
Must seek refuge in
Mystic Valley's cascading
Waterfall remained
Peaceful to dismiss
Any care in the world
Flowing from the *Water's Edge*

Personal mantras
Sparked a desire
To fulfill a wishful stroll
Within chosen daring individuals
Who've cared to watch
A *grieving & illuminating*
Reflection *manifest & unfold*
From the depths of every
Haunted & Lost soul
Who fell victim to being
Washed up along the *Water's Edge* shore

Was a mystified scene
Now forever etched within
The memories of witnesses a far
From conceptual normalcy
Yet haunting events
Would literally take
The breath away
From anyone
Daring enough to say
I know what it feels like
To be seen ***Living Near The Water's Edge***

THE WAKING HOUR
(VERSION 2)

The Waking Hour is an alibi
To cope with lost regrets
That pierce the soul
With *each* and *every*
Step taken a last breath
Could relinquish a proposed safe haven
If *The Waking Hour* came like a thief
In the night disguised as Satan
Deeming to be a soul taker
With the graciousness of a saint
Could now be seen as a patron
In the eyes of a world filled with

Bigamy and *Hatred*
Leaving belated deception
As the pointed finger
Needed to be used for *The Waking Hour*
Red flags were labeled within the minds
Of every *Waking* follower
Would remain the last seen
Alarm clocks left for saving
Each other from an untimely
Cast slaughter was
Yet to be visibly
Made *self-evident* & *piously* undone

PIT OF DECEPTION
(GETTING OUT OF IT)

Running in circles fast
I must reach
The top of a spiraled
Bottomless
Pit Of Deception
(Getting Out Of It)
Is easier said than done
The fear of losing a promising life
Kept mindful verging escape cycles
Perpetual enough for
Favoring *despair* and *condemnation*

Yet as I'm getting closer to
Reaching the brink of exhaustion
My last breath of desperation
Near the pit's top edge
Seems within the vicinity
Of reaching a believable lifelong freedom
Yet *(Getting Out Of)* this predicament
Defines a misconception of hope
Promoting no real chance
Of escaping this sound *Pit Of Deception's*
Grip on my savored fate

A Loving Memory Of Thy Lost Self's Virtue

What ever happened
To whom you
Once were some time ago?
After that new savvy attitude
Moved in by the waist side
Now making way
For what had to begin

As a vowed reconstructive thoughtful process
Renewed a grief-stricken
Cognition in vested ways
Forever taking the place
Of traced regrets
Discovering
A Loving Memory Of Thy Lost Self's Virtue

A Loving Memory Of Thy Lost Self's Virtue:

Chosen Whispers In The Wind (Original)

Don't look to intend on finding who you
Once knew during memorable times of
Festive convenience now remain in the
Shadows of your past's gold plated rearview
Mirror's insignia was placed aside
To *picture* & *remember* authentic
Sounds of friends who've now actualized being
A Loving Memory Of Thy Lost Self's Virtue:
Chosen Whispers In The Wind

REACHING FOR THE NEAR AFTER

As much as
It's anticipated
Everyone's **Reaching** grasp
Mirrors a yearning gasp
For a *near after* in contrast
With the *here* and *now*
Many invisible walls separate
Our vision and *Tangible desires*
For a sought-after prize

Appeared like
We're on the outside looking in on
Our ardent inclination's real
Center of attention still
Unveils blessed entities personifying
The need to perfect
Persona's addressed imperfections
Appeared in ***The Near After***
Seeking validation clues

Candle Blowers
(Dimeter Version)

Our living lights
Are the eyes of
A future now
Held high to fly
Should be set free
Like caged dreams seen
Blowing in the

Wind's trivial
Reality
A flaring wick's
Melting candle
Wax for our souls
Must make it past
An ongoing

Plethora of
Well-wishers in
Disguise as a
Waiting line for
The envious
Classless Masses'
Candle Blowers

DISHEARTENING ASSOCIATIONS

It's unfortunate
Being stabbed in the back
By a fellow acquaintance
In remembrance
Of a false friendship

Turned opportunistic
Always ruins
A valued perception
Of brethren companionship
Among us

Paints an unlikely portrait
Where trust issues
Are routinely exposed due to
The provocation of deep felt
Disheartening Associations

FANTASY'S BLINDING LIES
(TRIMETER VERSION)

Devoted emotions
From the vainness tree of
Tempted awakenings
Speared a controversy
Passionately beyond
Witnessed extremes had been
An undying beauty's
Silhouette did set up
A contemporary
Man's mind into a trance

Like state purposely saw
On the eve of his ball
Mistaking deception's
Vixen poison ivy
With the nature of his
Caring and *Radiant*
Wife's vanity bearing
Clear shields of trustworthy
Complexities from his
Fantasy's Blinding Lies

BEING ALONE IN A WORLD FULL OF PEOPLE
(REVISED)

How can we still be
Quarantined *spiritually* and *socially*
With so many people on the planet
As time runs rapid
Our personal ties
With history
As individuals

Will become evident
While the plight of our lives
Remains a present open book
That's unfolding *day in* and *day out*
It's interesting to think about
This universal link
Everyone can engage in

Nowadays this common link is envisioned
As a friendly conversation with
A people's mass majority not believing in
The notion that everyone is equal
In their own eyes
The morale for this
Social stock exchange has dropped beyond zero

As *More* and *More* people
Are becoming superficial beings
For wrongfully known popularity reasons
Throughout the seasonal course of today's framed timeline
In this game called life
Being Alone In A World Full of People
Comes with a familiar territory when it remains humanly trite

Hating A Part Of Ourselves We Can't Live Without

It's that genetic tendency
We can't shake
Habits & *Mannerisms* shape
A sure biological fate
Showcasing our *height* & *weight*
Today we fascinate the masses for certain

What we've gotten
From our parents started this inherited trend
With a unique hair color
Which attracts people to you
Those biological attitudes
Shown & *Seen* through a family name

Affiliated with a harsh temper
Exists within you as
A blend of two bloodlines
From each parent's side
Society loves to confide in
Those facial features

Like the *size* & *shape of your eyes, nose* and *ears*
You need them to *survive & live*
Among your peers within a world of prone uncertainties
Confirming that *fear, doubt, shame* and *viewed self-loathing*
Proves we're just fittingly
Hating A Part Of Ourselves We Can't Live Without for now

WINDS OF CONCEPTUAL CHANGE

A **Northwest** wind of ambition
Was ahead of an abstract thinking jet stream
At 60 mph
It seemed to be pervasively
Drifting a **Southwest** wind of indecision
Drew much attention to

A gusting **Westward** wind
Foreshortened
A *valid* & *discrete* social storm
Moved in a raining cultural norm
Changed the shape of
A *barring* & *crucial* cloud of impropriety's

Mission at hand appeared to be in demand
But an **Eastbound** wind was on the verge of
Guaranteeing a *definite end*
To the lasting effects
Warranting all the known
Winds Of Conceptual Change

WHY TURN YOUR BACK ON WHAT COULD BE?

It's engaging
As an epic portrait
Where the sight of
Monumental experience
Is worth capturing
Beyond its intricate meaning
Of self-importance
Yet in a split second
There's a decision to be made
Will you covet what's at stake?

Or

Will you have to many regrets?
Brought on by self-sabotage
Along with hesitant sole credibility
Why Turn Your Back On What Could Be?
Positively commencing in your life
As time ticks away
Towards an irrevocable fazed reality
Which can't be changed once our known
Mortal hourglass
Becomes depleted in due time

IF YOU COULD SPEED UP TIME

(WHERE ELSE WOULD YOU RATHER BE?)—PRELUDE

Like a remote
Controlling human objectivity
It would be a rare blessing in disguise
If You Could Speed Up Time
(Where Else Would You Rather Be?)
It's an intriguing question for anyone
Who's a true daydreamer at heart
Why befriend reality?

When life's pendulum
Is constantly *swinging* & *moving*
If You Could Speed Up Time
(What Else Would You Rather Be Doing?)
With your life if *the second* to *last line*
Was a preview of what's next to come
From within the confides
Of a poet's disclosed written mind

If You Could Speed Up Time

(What Else Would You Rather Be Doing?)—Conclusion

A previously
Intriguing question
From a promising prelude
Has opened up a suggestion box

In response to this peculiar motion
If You Could Speed Up Time
(What Else Would You Rather Be Doing?)
Within a constantly

Ever-changing world
Some like to work
Others love to gamble
Most advocate an aura of self-preservation

But this best notion of sorts
Varies from *person* to *person*
Hobbies lie quiescent within the center
Of each *heart's desires* & *devotional ties*

To the spirit of speeding up time
(What Else Would You Rather Be Doing?)
With your life since a coveted answer remains
Within this inquiring question

Why ask *Why?*
When it comes to seeking out a purposeful alibi
With what you're doing when trying to speed up your time
With relational destinies

HOW WOULD YOU LIVE IF YOU NEVER EXISTED?

(SCI-FI VERSION)

It's an intriguing question to date
Yet interesting enough to go into detail
About the unknown galaxies in space
Planetary voyages demonstrate
The illustration of a lifestyle
Humanized as an alien
Within their intergalactic space age in disguise
When linking to a populace that truly matters
Other alien life-forms are being subservient
To diverge social interactions
With the earthly beings chosen

To host a subverted space expansion
As gravity maintains proximity
Promoting *experimentation* and *procreation*
For a phased morphing cycle of evolution
The real but dramatized question is
Would you want to *live* and *exist*
As *an alien* or *an android*
Within their proposed features seen
In this closed galaxy
How Would You Live If You Never Existed?
(Sci-Fi Version)

The Elements
Of Life—Italicized

The Elements of Life
Keep me in stride
To embrace a beginning
Now revived on the inside of
My **Spiritual Furnace**
Fueled a wise **Burning Desire**
Consciously forever linked
To random conversations with
Daily strangers presented

A treasured **Camaraderie**
Among colleagues alike
Where **Hearsay** played a vocal part to ignite
The course of action for
Weather Predictions and
Money Transactions
Governed the usage of **Oxygen**
Substantiated an italicized reason to why
The Elements of Life

Remained a *bold* & *meaningful* link
For bringing me
Closer to the brink of **Veracity**
Where being **Socialistic**
Lead a spoken trail down a path
Found in valued solemnity
Stayed under *lock* and *key*
Within *sacred scripts* and *doctrines* for
The Elements Of Life

WORLD RENOWNED POETIC SEASONS OF CHANGE
(REVISED SEASONS OF CHANGE VERSION)

In the ***Fall***
I learned to crawl
As I came into the world
A beginner
When the following ***Winter***

Approached
I was in awe of what could've been possible for me
So then in the ***Spring***
I *grew* a little *taller* and *began listening*
To daily random conversations publicly

The wonderment of life was heard
Amongst the living mass majority
Of people who befriended me
While I peeked through a social window
Of an intriguing opportunity
So maybe later I could spread my best character wings

Fly away and *Become somebody*
In society
But then
Finally **<u>Summer</u>** decided
To *show itself* and *reign supreme*

Because the chance to become illustrious
As a world-renowned poet
Had occurred to me
Before my very own eyes
With perfected timing

There's A Better Place For Everyone

There's A Better Place
For *each* and *every* one of us
Where the atmosphere
Has no bearings on our destinies
As vested individuals
With chosen testimonies

Illuminated the spectrum
For center stage's
Grand ceremony
Inducted **Everyone** in the front row
Who believed in
Relatively speaking up for themselves

Attended entry into
"The Hall Of Infinite Possibilities"
Was a sound place for every human being
Wanting to experience
Their own **Grandiose Dreams** in grand fashion
As we speak on the terms of their discovered sanctuary

FEELING LIKE A FEATHER IN THE WIND
(TRIMETER VERSION)

Feeling Like A Feather
In The Wind innocence
Had chosen to lay its
Dear influential hand
On the appearances
Near a burdened shoulder's

Essence now mentioned the
Power vested in a
Loving heart's reach only
Can befittingly teach
Compassion to the likes
Of all maligned spirits

Who remain to stay on
The path of admired differences leading
To forgiveness beyond a redeemable age
Between *men* and *women*
Genuinely forthright correspondence bridges
Eccentricity's gaps

From the likes of beguiled
Individual worlds
Mirrored with vanities
Fueled by definitive
Curious conflicts of
Interests among their peers

BUDDING STARS WHO SHINE THE BRIGHTEST

A shooting star
Illuminates a darkened sky
By far
The sight of a blossoming talent
Is commemorating

Like a *Fourth of July* eye-opening
Fireworks celebration
Inspired the uninspired
Who were craving to know
Why they saw

Each talented newcomer
Deserved & Desired
To bear
Their own worthy flag's
Aspired significance

When it was called upon
A performing stage
For all to see masterful
Budding Stars Who Shine The Brightest
Within the spotlight of their best talents

When That Opportune Time Arrives

As the mind grows
In preparation towards
Strengthening ourselves for
A speculative tomorrow
Seconds will turn into *Minutes*
Minutes will turn into *Hours*
Hours will turn into *Days*
Days will turn into *Weeks*

Yet *Weeks* will turn into *Months*
As *Months* will turn into *Years*
When That Opportune Time Arrives
For spiritual revival
We shall fly away peacefully
Like doves without known earthly ties
To the *lies* & *compliances*
Of our estranged world

THERE'S A SILVER LINING IN EVERY DARK CLOUD

Watch out for those dark clouds
Hovering about
Looking to shower upon
Anyone who's living
Tumultuously happy

Beyond their means
While befriending
Their *daydreams* & *jubilant fantasies*
In splendid fashion
Life imitates art with a passion

So there's no stopping
An undying love for
Positivity, Extravagance, & Tranquility
Because in everyone's heart of hearts
There's A Silver Lining In Every Dark Cloud

POETRY

(FOREVER A POET'S BEST FRIEND TILL THE VERY END)

For **Poetry** there's no real way
To describe a poet's best friend from
Who's **Forever** defined as
A true comforter during lonely times
With penned evidence of *rhyme* or *reason*
During each season of a **Poet's** life
It's an advised demeanor
Turning all known *skeptics* into *believers*

Seen without voiced affiliations
Beyond lighting this ever-changing diction candle
There's a poet's vocal eternal flame
From within its complemented
Influence expresses
Why a star's talent shines brightly
Like spirited embodiments
Brought a poet *peace* and *solace*

When our society was too distant
And yet perplexing during bleak writing periods
Where no real companionship exists
With a poet's evolved *artistry* and *pen*
It's good to know
A loyal **Best Friend** is present
When word elements are
Protecting and *Encompassing* a known poet's self-made

Literary department in the name of camaraderie
Forever obtaining bonded equity during
Crucial times of emotional upheaval
Till The Very End of a poised poet's living journey
Wrote during life's frequented turbulences of
A questionable yet now defined durational growth period
For *each* and *every* existing
Poet on earth who's a messenger of hope in terms of forgotten souls

Preserve The Places You Love The Most

It's your favorite spot
In a park
You grew up near
Or it's a known tourist attraction
Where a special lasting memory
Was photographed with your peers
Each nostalgic place
Left behind enduring memories
Of blissful visioned occurrences

Existing as an appearance
Of profoundly significant views
Experienced every year
Within your *heart* & *mind*
When it's clear to celebrate why
Without question you're there
Just striving to
Preserve The Places You Love The Most
Where the future can repeat itself

AN IDEAL TRAILER FOR YOUR DESTINED FUTURE

It's the best preview
Anyone would've
Ever dreamt of seeing
It's you
Five years from now

In a revealing sense
Of the words
Personal change while
Enjoying a higher plateau
Befitting to engage in

This fifteen-second
Commercial spot ends
With a twist
On a desired fate
Rated five stars

Was this spectacular
Last screening
For what will mainly be seen as
The exclusive rights for
An Ideal Trailer For Your Destined Future

ONLY NEEDS TO APPEAR WHEN NEEDED

God comes into play
When what you
Need to happen
In a timely manner
Corresponds with a myth
Named synchronicity

When all else will not fail in it's entirety
Why would *anxiety*
Bear such meaningful weight
During life itself?
As personal echoes
For forecasted demands

Are clearly heard from the start
Of internal pleading
Pacified antidotes
Amid well known chaos
May not sugarcoat
A great persona's

Relief efforts style
By honing in on what
Only Needs To Appear When Needed
In plain view of
Daily redeeming miracles
Governed by heaven sky's

MOONLIGHT SOLACE

The *stars* & *constellations*
Shine bright
As the night sky
Comforts a weary soul
Behind closed doors
A savored gratuity force

Was felt like warming embraces
Meant to cure the curiosity
Consoling factor seen
Within nocturnal beings
Surrounding dusk havens
Where they *influenced* & *manifested*

Twilight acceptance
Speeches under
Nightly skylines
Celestial serenity
Was consciously known
As ***Moonlight Solace*** beamed

COSMIC INFATUATION

An unexplored terrain…
A maelstrom of energy
Infused by infinite light
Vibrant kaleidoscopes dancing
As their silhouettes fervently collide…
A portal harboring truth

Illuminating serenity in their cosmos
Revealing their secrets…
In the realm of dreams
On a cloud the Goddess sleeps
Imagination parallels reality
Embracing the spectrum of another universe…

Its name is transverse
With elements of a veering kingdom
Where a crowned cosmic king
Will emerge
After a dazzling kiss
Commences with his queen
To be
Delegating a commanding spectrum
As they both weather
Their own galaxy devotion of loving storms

He then brings forth
His lips as a kissing scepter
Marking inevitable change
As their amorous constellations
Shed light upon
The darkness of a secret
Deeply rooted
Within the heart
Of his treasured Goddess

Held above the clouds
As they're forever bonded
By an enchanting
Devoted source
Never virtually known
By mankind as a whole

RAPTURE...INTERRUPTED
(UPON HER EMPTY PILLOW)

I told my love while dreaming
In a soft whisper of the early morning
As a half-light stirred
A threatening slow pleasure
Since dawn would wish to hurry…

If I could turn back time, love,
I would eclipse this sunlight with a wink
Embracing each moment
Safely within your warm arms
Of dreams that linger

Forever awakening in a sense
Of lost ravenous intentions
As a **Rapture… Interrupted**
A beloved stream of consciousness
In the mind of her love
Who cherished romantic sunsets

After taking her breath away
With his valiant efforts of devoted pleasure
It's a shame this rendezvous had come to an end
Within his passionate fantasy
(Upon Her Empty Pillow)

ANTECEDENT LOVE

It remained
A confidant
During a past life
No one wanted to let go
Of this rich **Antecedent Love**
Which
Nourished the unadorned
Depths of graced lovingness

With all committed souls
Who'd been seen
Entwined with *heartfelt* & *loving joy*
Basked in pure devotion of the moonlight
Congenial love potion
Will always be
An unforgettable urge
To be worth more than genuine designating assumptions

For all who've chosen the path
At regaining a lost sense
Of endearing personal happiness
Which made a brief presence now
During every affected person's
Devoted and *Short* love life
All loving minds know
Short love lives are a savored past time's prize

Is There Really One True Love For Each Of Us All?

Where's that one true love for each of us all?
This mounting anticipation
Serves as an indication
Like receiving an unexpected phone call
Out of the blue

Every heart yearns for a devoted loving acceptance
Backed by doting chemistry revealed
Where a dear *couple's intent* and *caring tendencies*
For one another
Was meant to be *tried* and *true* by

Strengthened meaningful unions
In progress even as the world turns
With or *Without* stress
No more or *No less* than
The number of vast forgotten singles

Who've been looking to seal the leaks
On board their love ship's vessel at sea
Raised each of the lonesome deck hands
Heart-aching eyebrows who were
Pleading to *see* and *experience*

Beyond love's wall of begotten infidelity
Sheds light on this absolutely raised question
Merely in all reality
Is There Really One True Love For Each Of Us All?
Who're single with charm

THE NEXT
LOVING GARDENER
(SHORT VERSION)

Men should treat women
Like lovely flowers
Favoring affection showers
As often as possible
Neglecting their fragile emotional needs
Could turn your relationship

Into a perennial mystery
So giving light emotionally
In the form of a gesture
Praising their radiant beauty
Could only prevent
A passionate rooted escape

From *happening* & *seeing*
Your womanly rose petals
Leaving you all alone
To be cared for by
The Next Loving Gardner
Who's seized your lost love

FORTITUDE BLISS

Her love became
Addictive like
A drug unheard
Of to a man's

Words seen written in
Plain English since
Possessiveness was a dearly cherished
Bond's last passionate kiss when a favored night's

Romantic touch
Sparked a heartfelt crush as
Transpired love feelings
Often were passive enough to become voiced

Decadence as her spirited
Nectar brought boldly
Devotional tendencies to life
With loving wishes extending a ***Fortitude Bliss***

DIRECTIONAL EPIPHANIES

Figurative hunches
Have set sail
On the vast surface of oceanic currents
Waves of detailed revelations
Are not clichés
Since tomorrow's yesterdays

Will be gone forever
While blowing
Within the waved winds of
Destined and *Vocally* chosen
Directional Epiphanies
Dreamt Views

VISIONED NOVELTY DREAMS

Personal shelves
Longing with thoughts
Remain preserved
Near sealed labels
Seen on past years
Jars with valued

Question marks basked
In the shadows
Drawn are consent
Regards shackled
By misfortune
Silhouettes masked

With dark vapor
Flared consciousness
Was involved in
Jet streams highlight
Reality
Opposed *Visioned Novelty Dreams*

Why Do We Waste So Much Time In Our Lives?

Seconds
Minutes
Hours
Days
Months
And more years to come

Different *faces* and *generations*
Are still in a hurry to fulfill their fixation
With wasting time
The trade-off to get ahead
In our prime stayed popular as a crazed illusion
Displayed meaningful forgone conclusions

Of people
In a rush to get too nowhere
In particular
Yet we love to *stop* and *stare*
At the constantly moving hands
On the clock

Tick tock, Tick tock
As we *witness* and *watch*
Our intangible hard-fought concerns
Clearly focused on due diligence
In a hazed fashion mainly underlies
Perception's trivialities with how and
Why Do We Waste So Much Time In Our Lives?

Spiritual Love

A genuine piece
Of framed artwork
Shows us at peace with
The *heavens* and *below*
Daily and *Nightly* skies
Lies deafening uncertainty was not
Uncommon to the nature of mankind's

Curiosity within our mind
Dwells and *Urges* us to *Seek* and *Find*
Why we must spread our savored wings of gratitude
Like a dove in search of its *meaningful* and *joyed*
Blessings governing our need for sacred
Spiritual Love bonds
Addressed here on earth

HEALING FROM SELF-SABOTAGE

Self-inflicted wounds
Hurt the most
When we're moving forward
With our efforts
To join in on
A grand toast

For coming close
To partaking in
Our self-envisioned future's
Last present time's spin on life
Shattered a mirrored view
Of many blessings

Cut off
From **Self-Sabotage** recipients
Was our *divine* & *giving* true self
We'd personally love to hear **From**
Once sensed **Healing** dissipates fate
In disguise as the heights at which we fell from grace

Hidden Under
The Light Of Day
(Version 3)

The light of day *comes* and *goes*
Unnoticed within the eyes
Of fantasy goers alike
A drawn mirage of volition
Remains hidden inside daylight's sunrays
Of *warmth* and *hopefulness* for a better tomorrow
The treasures of the unseen
Are hard to be seen once behind the eyes

Of sole *skeptics* and carelessly speaking *beings*
Revel in the inconvenience
Of not finding what is meaningful
Within their hearts of desperation
They want activation
Of their morality's checkpoints
Without further hesitation while they've been
Deceived to believe in a dream

Focused on finding meaning
In the occurrences of lost causes
Along the way towards deliverance
Now remains after the last disappointments of gone yesterdays
Already happened without *warning* or *delay*
For the sake of self-preservation
Which has currently been
Hidden Under The Light Of Day

Is the vague way
To display
What's within the foray
Of a lost definitive soul's gazed
Daylight shadow to date
Illustrates a puzzling spectacle
Meant to start demonstration's
Written art imitating life

NIGHTLY SHADES

A calming refuge
Within the twilight
Peacefulness gives birth
To insight unseen
By the naked eye
Dusk draws its curtain
Attention over viewed open window's
Darkened glass frames made

Savvy escapades
Shield and *Save* us from drama
Uncommon to most souls
Is veiled like pupils
Fixed with dormant nocturnal
Instincts played villain
Unveiled while wearing
Optic ***Nightly Shades***

STEALING HAPPINESS FROM CHOSEN SECONDS OF A MOMENT'S TIME FRAME

Who would ever complain about
Losing out
On any aspect of life
As long as we conduct ourselves
In a civil manner
On the account of meekness acts
Forecast
Selfishness
Would become lies

Towards a less painful truth
Where vanity has now become
A destitute factor
Used to inch most of us closer
Into plain view
Of what our lives
Could resemble
Once we're in the midst
Of greener pastures soon

Within our finest hour it's likely
Stealing Happiness From Chosen Seconds
Of A Moment's Time Frame
Remains a coveted myth
For what
Lies ahead
Within the future life
Lessons our past lives
Had taught us since the beginning
Of our livelihoods

Father Time Will Eventually Catch-Up With Us All

As good as it gets in this life
Father Time
Transcends lone evolution
Despite relapses in
Our own heart of desire
For making every special dream
Comply to be

Relevant and *Apparently*
Before the clock of ages
Reaches *midnight* after *dark*
Father Time stretched self-limits
Of personal bias
By turning us into purposed reminders
When exposing light on

What will be
Only after the sole preview
Precedes the show's screening
Soon reveals
What's next to come
Like a rare butterfly
Who began its amazing life as an intriguing caterpillar cocooned

PLAY YOUR PART IN THE GRAND SCHEME OF LIFE

Everyone has a role
To play
In this *day* & *age*
The question is
Will you take
Your starring role
During the season
Of your life's sitcom?
Where the reward for this pilot

Is classic syndication
Forever it outweighed
Being *canceled* & *placed*
Inside your minds memorabilia vault
Where cherished reruns
Revive virtuous dreams
Of this *personated & treasured* success theme
Remember to
Play Your Part In The Grand Scheme Of Life

APPRECIATE GOOD DAY FORTUNATE WHEN IT HAPPENS

It's that sigh of relief
When you've made it
Through a long stretch
Of relentless disbelief
Your heart's been
Pounding for awaited signs
Mirroring the best miracle

Falling from the sky
It's amazing *how* & *why*
A divine order
Complies with grace
Daily chaos makes us
Appreciate Good Day Fortune When It Happens
In a timely fashion

EMOTIONAL REPRIEVE

We're tired of
Wearing our own hearts
On our sleeves
Just to fake
Being seen emotionally free
With ease
What we all need

Is a chance to find
A retreat in life
Disguised as a feat
Towards obtaining
A morale boosting
Emotional Reprieve
Within the confines of our soul's sanctuary

A Toast To New Beginnings

The remnants
Of a forgotten setback's
Alias were eliminated
From the consciousness of victims
Caught in a broad net
Of their own chosen disappointments

Since a smile means
A lot more to someone
Who's overcome their monotony
Branded by daily trivial pursuits
Followed a winning suit
Shown as playing card hands

Involved in
Personal happiness virtues
Meant to exceed
Our chanced *expectations* and *views*
Of modern-day stresses
Mediating our world today

Served all beneficiated purposes
For giving us
Second and *Third*
Rare chances towards the privileged
Sought after vocalized advocacy of
A Toast To New Beginnings

APPRECIATING THE OPEN ROAD'S VAST TRAVELS

It's a special freedom
A few will relish to
Admit the benefits
Of experiencing
Such an event
Traveling at a *fast* & *vivid* pace
With the wind blowing
In a jubilant face
Of traveled contentment
Remains an
Endeared close preview for

What each fine heart desires
Since the wonderment of life
Is felt
By every soul-searching driver
Who's first tried approaching a
Great and *Thoughtful* beginning
Of a *forever*-and-a-*day* journey
Yet it will only commence
When our driver's morale for now
Indefinitely starts
Appreciating The Open Road's Vast Travels

A CALMING BREEZE
OF SERENITY

I love feeling the serenity
Of a *cool* & *gentle* breeze
Across my cheeks
I sought *solace & peace* from
A Calming Breeze Of Serenity
Made *intuitive* & *gracious*

Revelations worth experiencing
As this reassuring wind of personal truth
Brought forth a revealing
Serene sanctity into fruition
After I've gazed at the sun
With my heart in sync

With the world before me
It's reassuring to know
Life's very meaningful
To live as long as
You're in touch with
Your unrevealed self

Then the world's mysteries
Will never remain
Hidden, Secretive, or *Forbidden*
Once they've been found
From within
The lone depths of your treasured soul

DRIFTING AWAY INTO A MELODIC ABYSS

It's that type of tune where life's troubles can't resume
As weary seasons of disgrace assume to grasp
Attention spans of each skeptic on the brink of

Evoking chaos into reality
Harmonious antidote's must persist as a
Witnessed serenade heard near the self-governed edge

Of yesterday's gleeful tall bridge were *harbored* souls
Who had endlessly savored real momentous bliss by
Drifting Away Into A Melodic Abyss

A New Found Innocence

A freed feeling came over
Every estranged human being
After the sky serenaded them
With purified raindrops of serenity
Washed away
All alarming memories
Of *hopelessness* & *despair*
Once a chance to *feel* & *witness*
This special experience came
Optimism opened
A reveled window of desired dreams

Forever introduced
A refreshed sense
Of spiritual renewal
Stepped on the scene
Fittingly
Everyone now knew
A New Found Innocence
Could be made possible
While making
Lasting & *Esteemed* bonds
With unpredictable Mother Nature

BREEZES OF AFFINITY
(SPECIAL 7 VERSION)

Becoming one with nature's
Abundant cycle broadcasts
Extravagant renewal
Social storms in common with
Everyone who's perceptive
With views in the atmosphere
Are clues binding our earthly

Original state beyond
The scope of our transcendence
Bears chosen affiliates
Whether *vocal* or *viral*
Lies complexity's social
Bond breathes within *you* and *me*
Breezes Of Affinity

Ocean Bliss

Along the shorelines of hopeful dreams
These breathtaking beaches set
The stage for an ***Ocean Bliss***
As infinite views of the tide came in
By washing away the disappointments
Of *well-wishers* and *bad intentions*

Of non-environmentalists
Along the shorelines of an ocean advocate's
Blissful beach sands remain to be seen for
Protecting wildlife
Along the world's seashores
Becoming an ally for all sea turtles

Crawling to be swept up in an ***Ocean Bliss***
They value the tide's strength
For keeping its rare species from becoming extinct
A special gift indeed brought forth from the heavens
Seen as a harmonious treasure
For sea world inhabitants

THE CALMING SHADE
(METERED VERSION)

Shadows hidden among daily
Extinction keep serenity's
Detailed secrets locked away in
Subconscious concealments vague to
Reality's endearments where

Man can find solace if its keys
Remain unlocked from all dreamlike visions
Meant to witness the fate of an
Unseen pastime now seen wistfully
Dreary in the daily mind's eye where

Nightfall's blissed storms made rare daylight mesh
With night to become one as life
And death unfolds in presence of
The Calming Shade's best concealed susceptive force's
Disguised undertakings

WRITTEN BEAUTY

(HAIKU)

Gracious rose petals
Dance a ballet in the wind
An exquisite scene

An Eyeful Reflection
Of Lives Past
(Poem Within A Poem Version)

All eyes were laid upon mindful shores
Named jubilation welcomed
An Eyeful Reflection Of Lives Past
Started calm *in the hearts and minds*
Of thoughtfulness pondered life's occasional tide
Came and went from what's dear to one's spirited soul
Partnered *with nostalgia's waves*
Made lasting *memories ageless yet*
Sacred along their fruitful visions *shoreline*
Footprints were in unison with the *sunrises and sunsets*
Of past lives *chaptered as silhouettes*